A Gerre Hancock Organ Album

MUSIC DEPARTMENT

OXFORD
UNIVERSITY PRESS

Great Clarendon Street, Oxford OX2 6DP,
United Kingdom

Oxford University Press is a department of the University of Oxford.
It furthers the University's objective of excellence in research, scholarship,
and education by publishing worldwide. Oxford is a registered trade mark of
Oxford University Press in the UK and in certain other countries

First published 2022

Impression: 1

ISBN 978-0-19-355229-6

Music and text origination by Andrew Jones
Printed in Great Britain on acid-free paper by
Caligraving Ltd, Thetford, Norfolk

Contents

Introduction

Born in Lubbock, Texas, in 1934, Gerre Hancock remained a proud Texan even as his career took him northwards. A graduate of the University of Texas and Union Theological Seminary in New York, he also studied at the Sorbonne; he took organ lessons with E. William Doty, Robert Baker, Jean Langlais, and Marie-Claire Alain, and studied composition and improvisation with Nadia Boulanger and M. Searle Wright. Early in his career he was Assistant Organist at St Bartholomew's Church, New York, and then Organist and Choirmaster at Christ Church (now Cathedral) in Cincinnati, Ohio, where he also served on the Artist Faculty of the College-Conservatory of Music at the University of Cincinnati; he also taught at the Juilliard School and Yale University. For thirty-three years, from 1971 to 2004, he was Organist and Master of Choristers at St Thomas Church, Fifth Avenue, New York, after which he and his wife, Judith Hancock, returned to Texas to teach the organ and sacred music at the University of Texas.

A superb recitalist, Gerre Hancock was considered the leading American organ improviser of his time and performed at numerous events worldwide, as well as achieving widespread acclaim with the choir of St Thomas. His improvisational and compositional style displayed a strong French influence while remaining grounded in a distinctively American musical vocabulary.

I first encountered Gerre Hancock's service-playing during the summer of 1970 at Christ Church in Cincinnati, and it opened my teenage ears to what service-playing could truly be. That same summer Gerre made his first commercial recording of improvisations, on the large 1957 Holtkamp organ which was then in Christ Church. Clarity, inventiveness, and variety of texture make these concise pieces models of hymn-based improvisation. After hearing them for the first time in many years, Judith Hancock remarked on their youthful freshness. Gerre's death in 2012 prompted me to finally transcribe a few of these gems, and I am delighted at their inclusion as a 'bonus feature' in this volume, which brings much of Gerre's published organ music back into print under one cover. I recorded the *Three Cincinnati Improvisations* on the superb Murray Harris organ at St James Episcopal Church in Los Angeles (Gothic G-49330-31, double CD).

In 2013 I had the privilege of recording all of Gerre Hancock's published organ works on the organs (chancel and gallery) that he played for so many years at St Thomas (Raven OAR-951, double CD). In the words of Judith Hancock, 'Years from now, when the organ heard on this recording is no longer at St Thomas, this CD will assist our memory of the uniquely thrilling and beautiful sounds of that instrument—sounds that were so closely associated with Gerre's own playing and composing.'

I hope you will find the music in this book both practical and educational in providing a window into the unique musical style of its composer. Gerre Hancock will be remembered by all who knew him as friend, mentor, inspiration, and ultimate cheerleader for church musicians across America and around the world.

TODD WILSON
Trinity Cathedral, Cleveland, Ohio
September 2021

for Judy

Air

A Prelude for Organ

GERRE HANCOCK

Sw.: Solo 8'
Gt.: Foundations 8', 4'
Ch.: Flutes 8', 4'
Ped.: Soft 16', 8', Ch. to Ped.

Slowly and sustained ♩ = *c.*72

Sw. ***mp***

Ch. ***p***

4

10
Ch.
Sw.
13
16
Gt.
mf
+ Gt. to Ped.
20
Add

24
Add f
Add ff
27
Ch. mf
Gt.
30
ritard.
Ch.
+ Full Ped.
Firmly and more slowly
ritard. greatly
33
Gt. fff Full Organ
reduce
p
- Gt. to Ped.

As at first
37
Sw. Soft Reed 8'
p
Ch. Strings, Flutes, Celestes 8'
pp
Flute 4' only
p
42
Ch.
reduce
pp
- Flute 4'
+ Soft Reed 4'
47
52
ritard.
- Reed 4'
+ Soft 16', 8'
+ Soft 32'

Dedicated to Jane and Ben Baldus
on the occasion of their twenty-fourth wedding anniversary

A Meditation on 'Draw Us in the Spirit's Tether'

Based on a melody by Harold W. Friedell

GERRE HANCOCK

I: Foundations 8', 4', III/I
II: Solo 8'
III: Foundations 8'
Ped.: Foundations 16', 8', III/Ped., I/Ped.

10
13
16
I *f*
+ I to Ped.
19
slowing
In time
I, III + Foundations 16', 8', 4', 2'
Mixture, Reeds 16', 8', 4'
f
Foundations 16', 8', 4', Reed 16'

22
25
28
Broadening
ff
I, III Reduce to Foundations 8'
mf
Reduce to Foundations 16', 8'
31
In time
slowing to the end
II Solo 8'
mp
III Reduce to Foundations 8'
p
Reduce to Flute 16', 8'
p

for The Rev. Robert Scoggin
and the Fellowship of United Methodist Musicians

A Paraphrase of 'St Elizabeth'

GERRE HANCOCK

I: Solo Flute or Flutes
II: Solo Stop
III: Soft Foundation 8' (Celestes)
Ped.: Soft 16', 8'

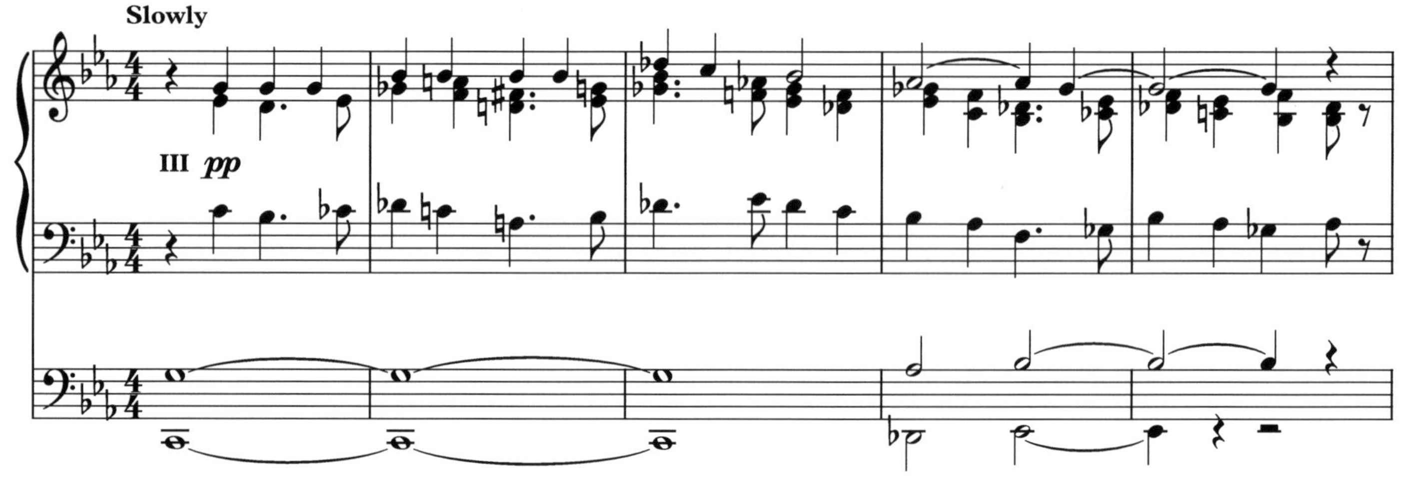

14
18
slowing
Tempo I
22
II + Foundations 8', 4'
II mf
sempre cresc.
mf
27
slowing

Tempo I

32 **+ Mixture & Reeds, II/I**

II/I ***f***

+ Mixture & Light Reed 16'

35

38

41

44
ff

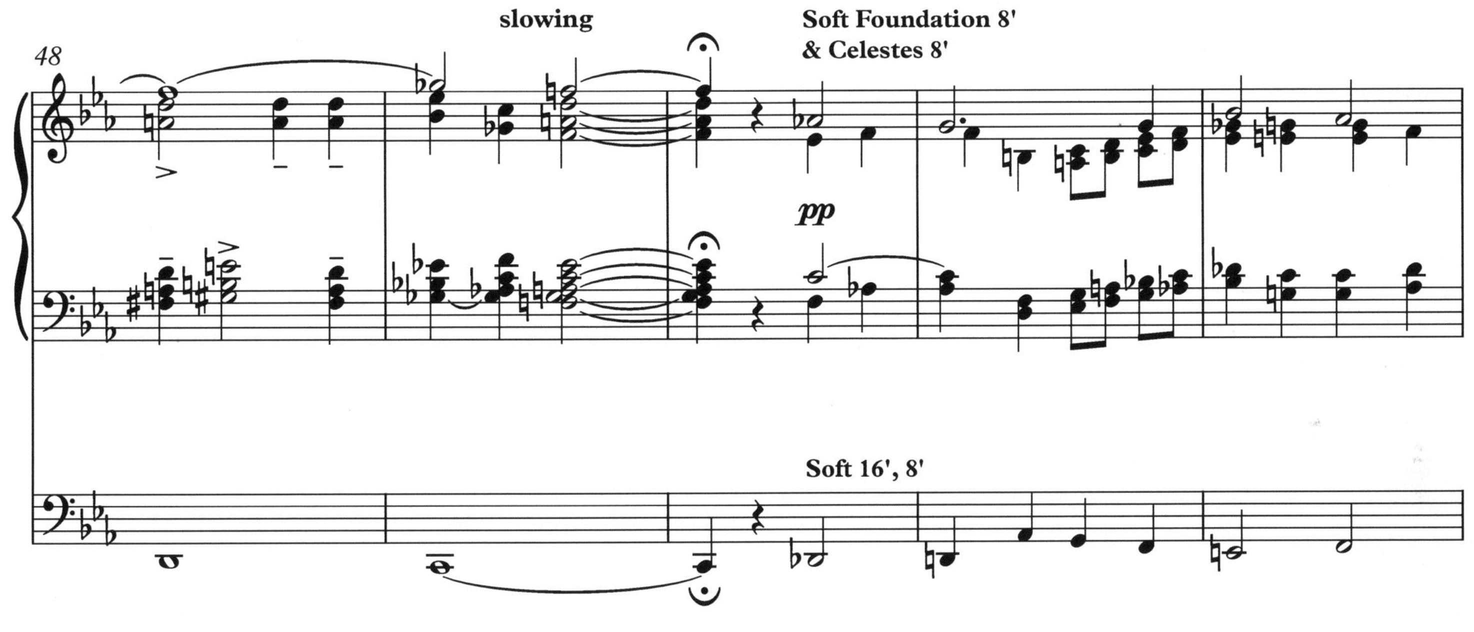
48
slowing
Soft Foundation 8'
& Celestes 8'
pp
Soft 16', 8'

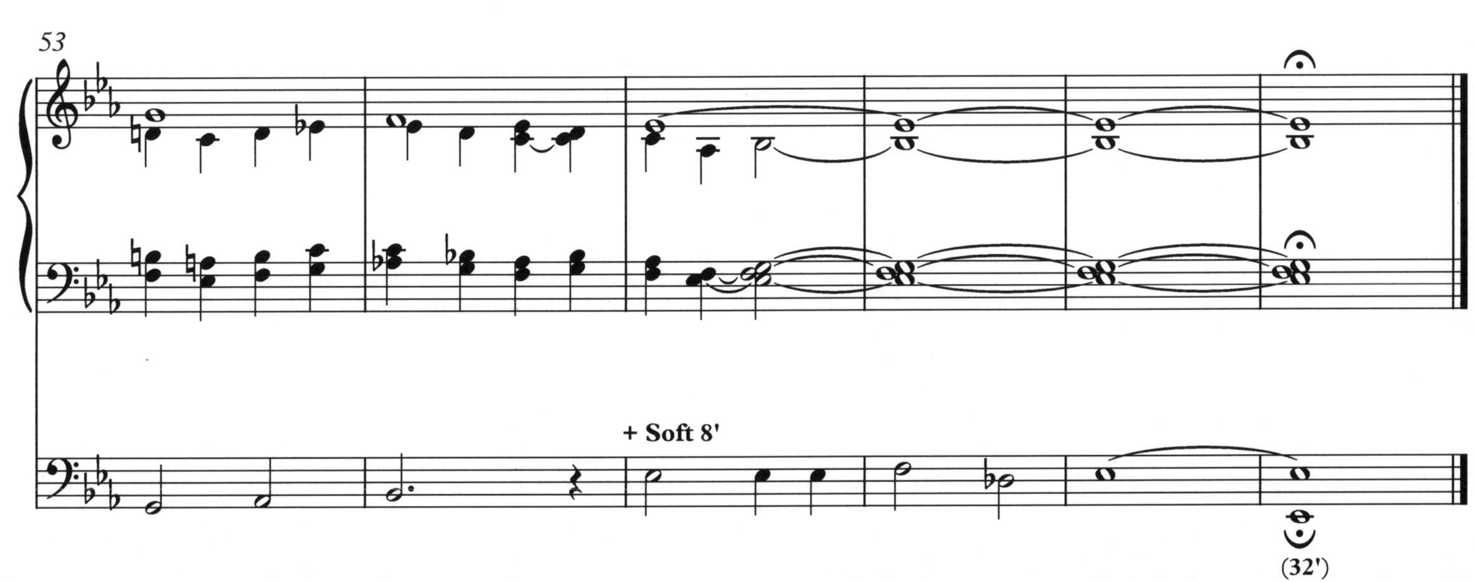
53
+ Soft 8'
(32')

Fanfare on 'Antioch'

('Joy to the world')

GERRE HANCOCK

19
24
rit.
a tempo
28
Solo Reed
33

to Robert Stevens Baker

Prelude on 'Slane'

GERRE HANCOCK

I: Foundations 8', 4', III/I, II/I
II: Foundations 8', 4'
III: Foundations 8', 4'
Ped.: Foundations 16', 8', III/Ped., II/Ped.

20
25
29
33

38
43
48
slowing
53
In time
f III + Reeds and 16'
II + Reeds and 16'
+ Foundation 32'

59
I + Reeds
and 16'
ff
64
slowing
I - Reeds
II - Reeds
III - Reeds
70
Slower
I, II, III
Foundations 16', 8' only
p
p
- 32'
p
75
pp

Commissioned by St Paul's School, Brooklandville, Maryland, for the dedication of the Schoenstein Organ in St Paul's Chapel on 10 November 2002

Toccata

GERRE HANCOCK

I: Foundations 8', 4', III/I, II/I
II: Foundations 8', 4', III/II
III: Foundations 8', 4', Reeds 8'
Ped.: Foundations 16', 8', III/Ped., II/Ped.

16
19
22
25
p
III
mp
28

31
34
37
40
III
43
II
mp
p

46
- II/Ped.
p
49
51
III
(III)
+ II/Ped.
mp
53

55
57
59
61
III
63
I
mf
II
mp

66
69
71
mp
73
75

77
79
II
mp
I
mf
mp
81
83
III
p
II
mp
+ I/Ped.
mf

85

87
mp
mf

89
mf
f

91

93
95
broadening
III + 16', 2 2/3', 2', Mixture
97
slowing
In time
99
III + Reeds 16', 4'
f
II +2 2/3', 2', Mixture
f
101

103
Ped. + 4', Reeds 16'
f
105
107
109

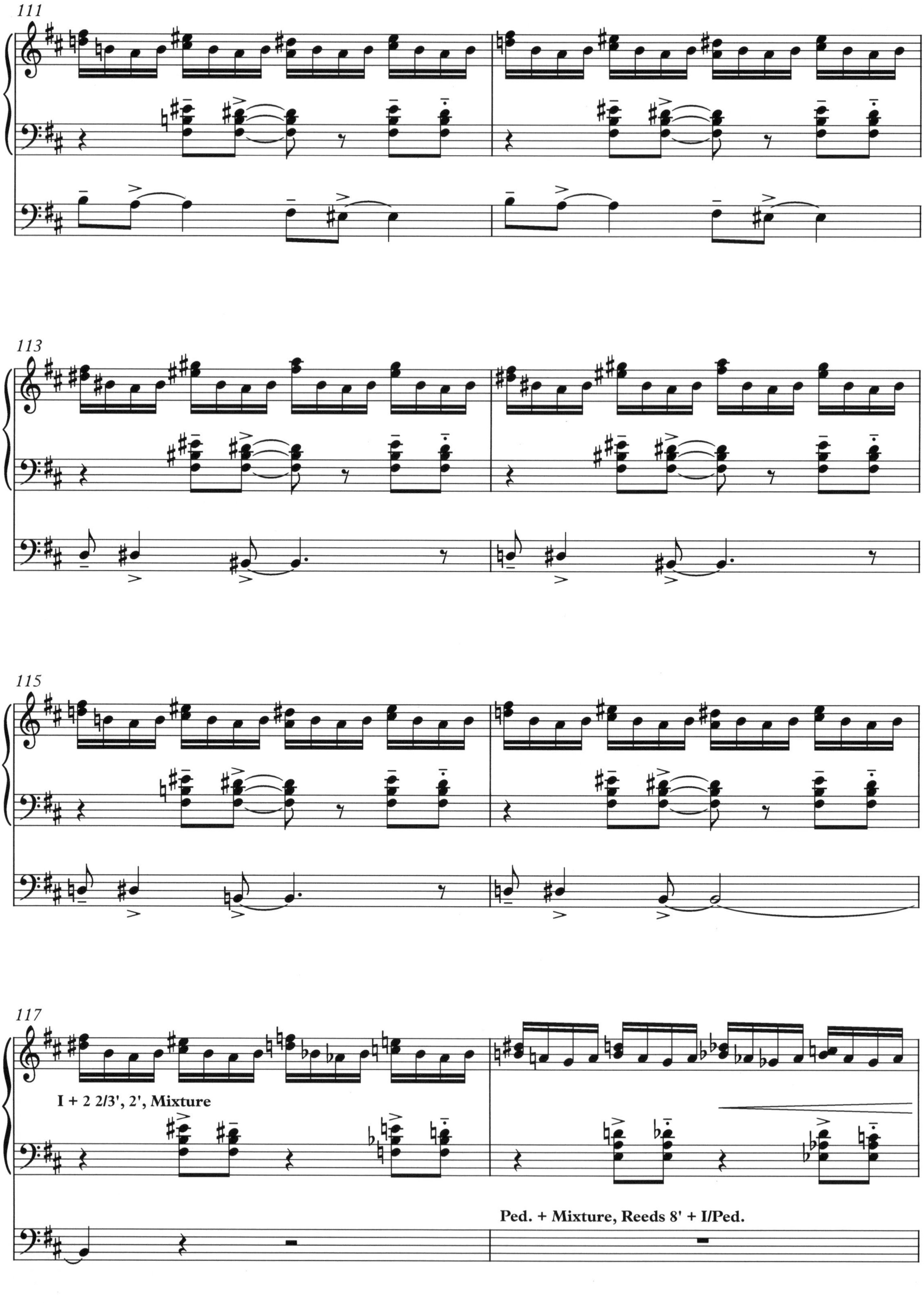
111
113
115
117
I + 2 2/3', 2', Mixture
Ped. + Mixture, Reeds 8' + I/Ped.

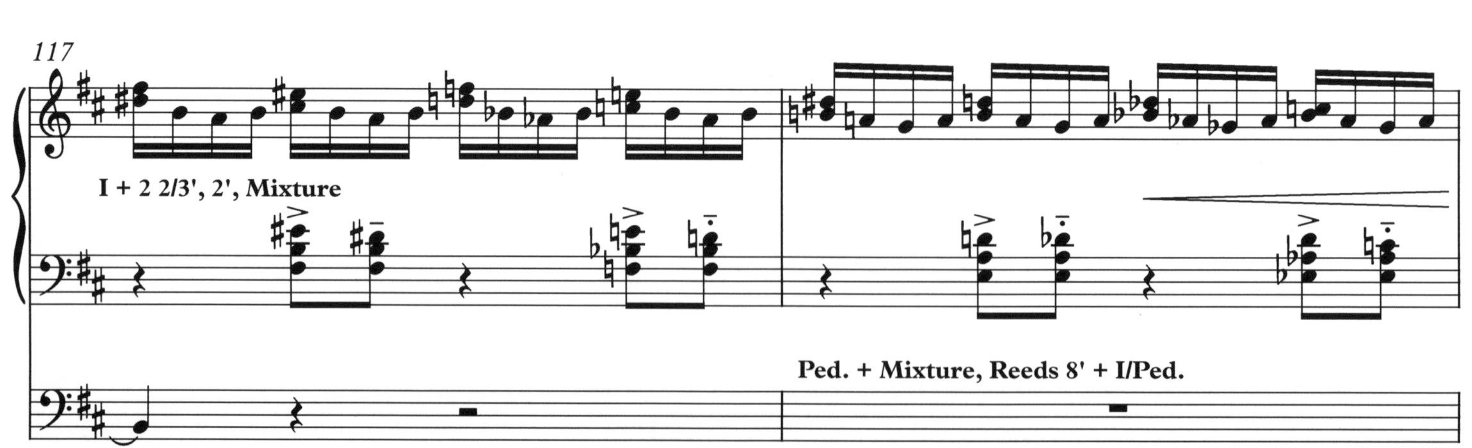

119
II + Reeds 16', 8'
ff
I
well detached

121

123

125

127
slowing
129
In time
ff well detached
I + Reeds 8'
ff
132
134

136
138
140
142

144
146
slowing
A little slower ♩ = c.112
fff Full Organ
Full Pedal
148
150
slowing
A little slower ♩ = c.104

152
154
slowing
In time
156
158
drive to the end

in memoriam Lewis Bruun

Variations on 'Ora Labora'

(Based on a hymn tune by T. Tertius Noble)

GERRE HANCOCK

I: Foundations 16', 8', 4', III/I, II/I
II: Foundations 16', 8', 4', Reed 8'
III: Foundations 16', 8', 4', Reed 8'
Ped.: Foundations 32', 16', 8', 4', Reeds 16', 8', III/Ped., II/Ped.

I

I: Solo 8'
III: Flutes 8'
Ped.: Flutes 16', 8'

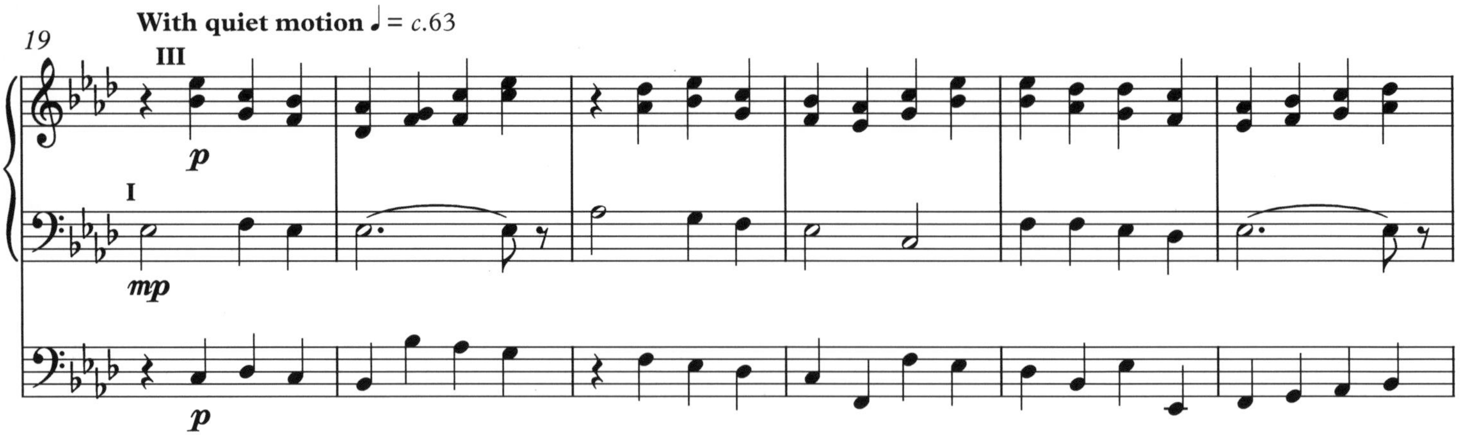
With quiet motion ♩ = c.63
19
III
p
I
mp
p

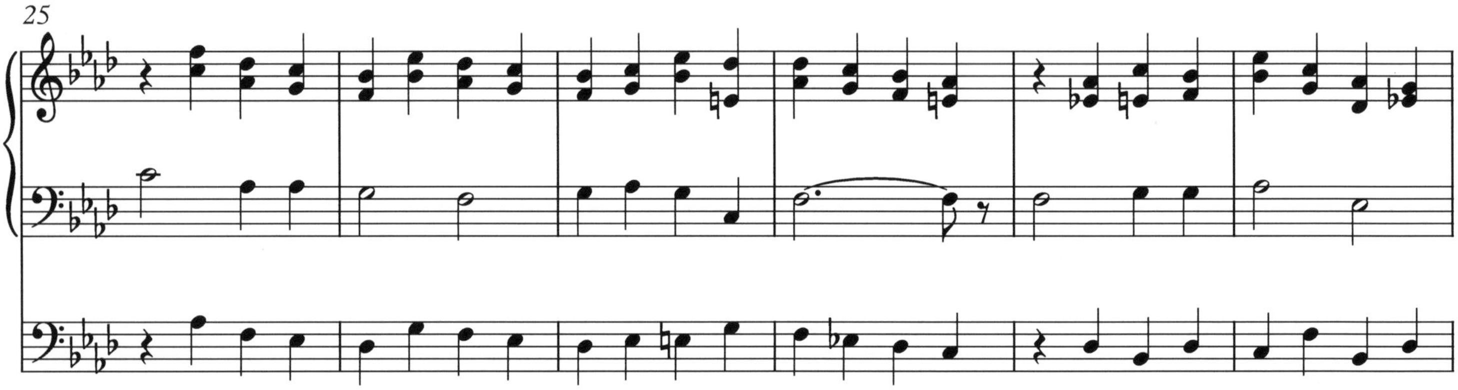
25

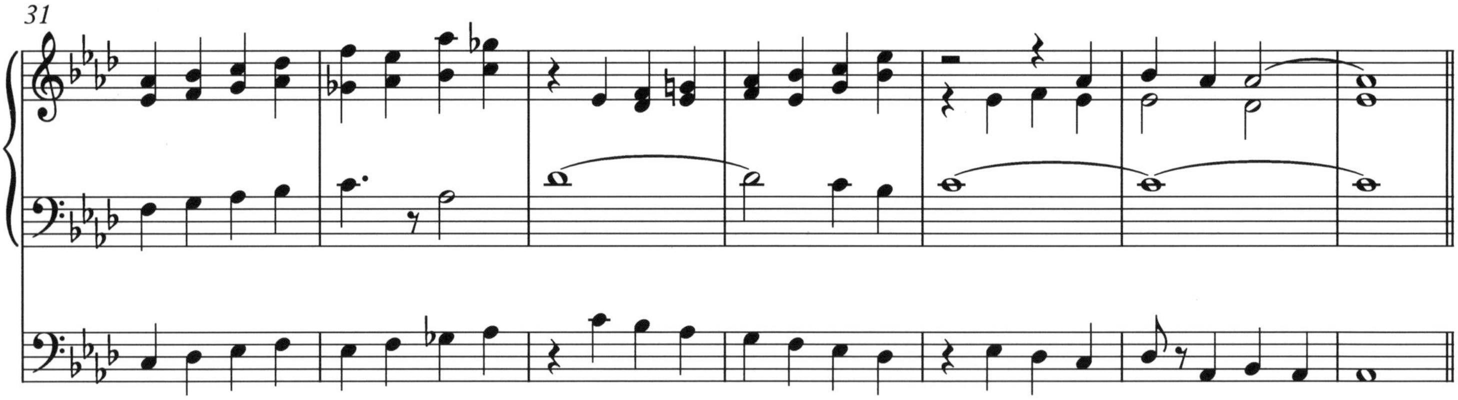
31

II

I: Flutes 16', 8'
III: Flutes 8', 4'

Lively and whimsically ♩ = c.96
38
III
Man. p
I

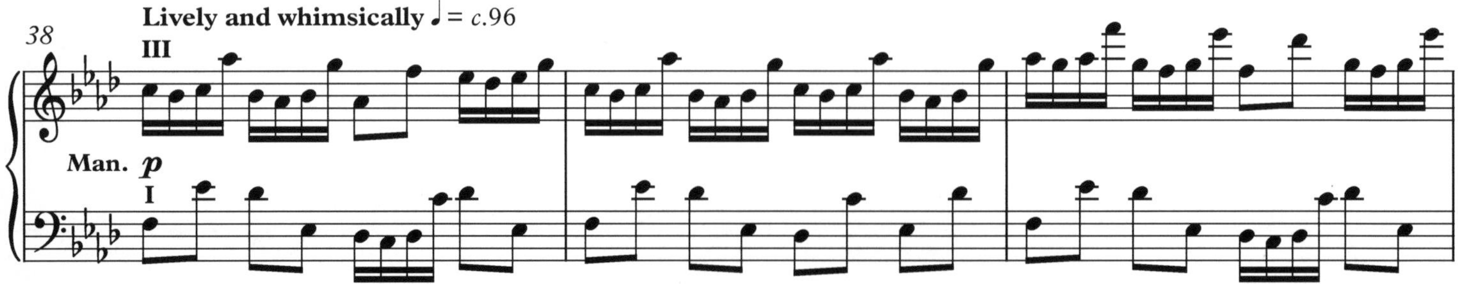

41
44
47
50
53
56

III

I: Flutes 8', III/I, II/I
II: Flutes 8', 4'
III: Flutes 8', 4'
Ped: Solo 8'

59 **Quickly and lightly** ♩. = *c.*92

I *mf*

f

62

66

70

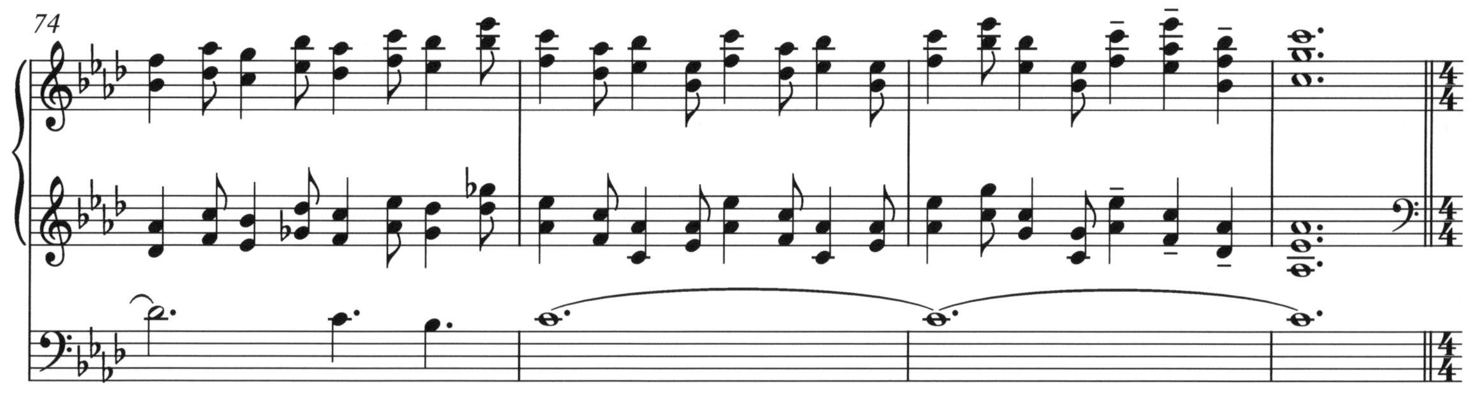

IV

II: Solo
III: Foundation 8'
Ped: 16', 8'

Slowly and langourously ♩ = *c.*52

78 II *mp* III *p* *p*

84

90

V

I: Foundations 16', 8', 4', Reeds 16', 8', III/I, II/I
II: Foundations 16', 8', 4', Reeds 16', 8', 4'
III: Foundations 16', 8', 4', Reeds 16', 8', 4'
Ped.: Foundations 32', 16', 8', 4', Reed 16', 8', III/Ped., II/Ped.

109
112
115
118
add fff
add fff
slowing to the end
123

Commissioned by the Association of Anglican Musicians Conference
and dedicated to the AAM 2000 Palm Beach Conference

Palm Beach

Hymn 777.777

Latin, 12th-century
Edward Caswall, trans.

GERRE HANCOCK

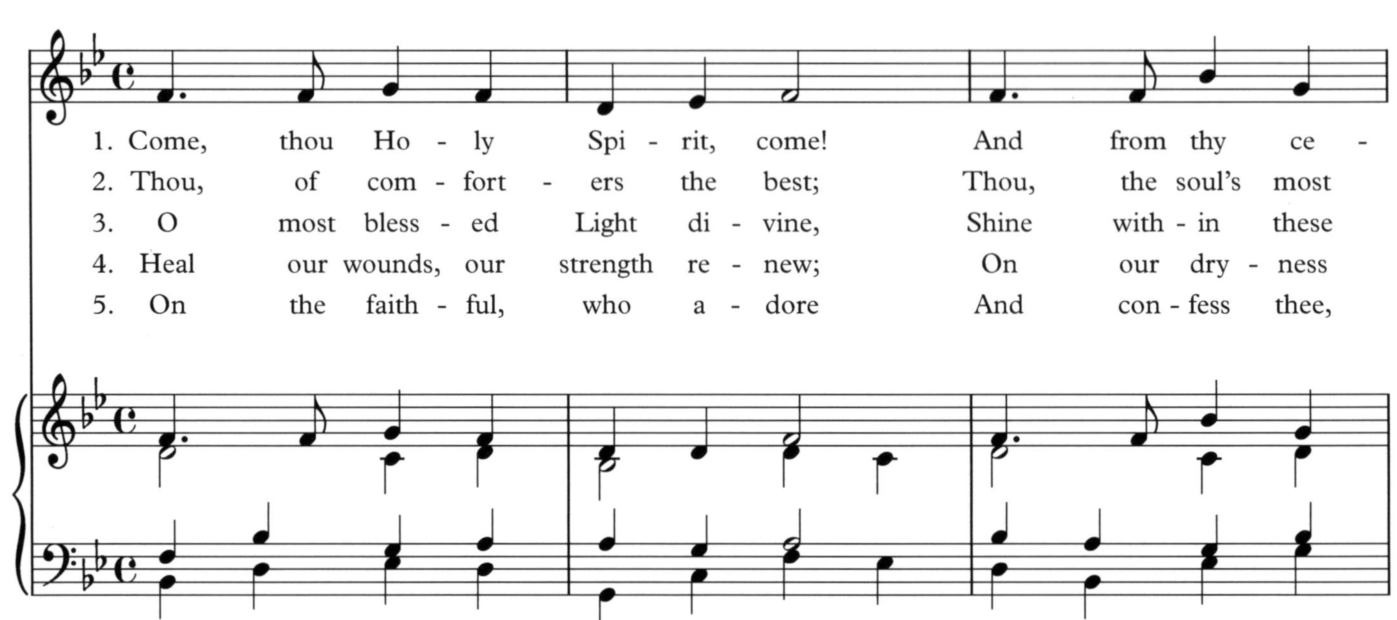

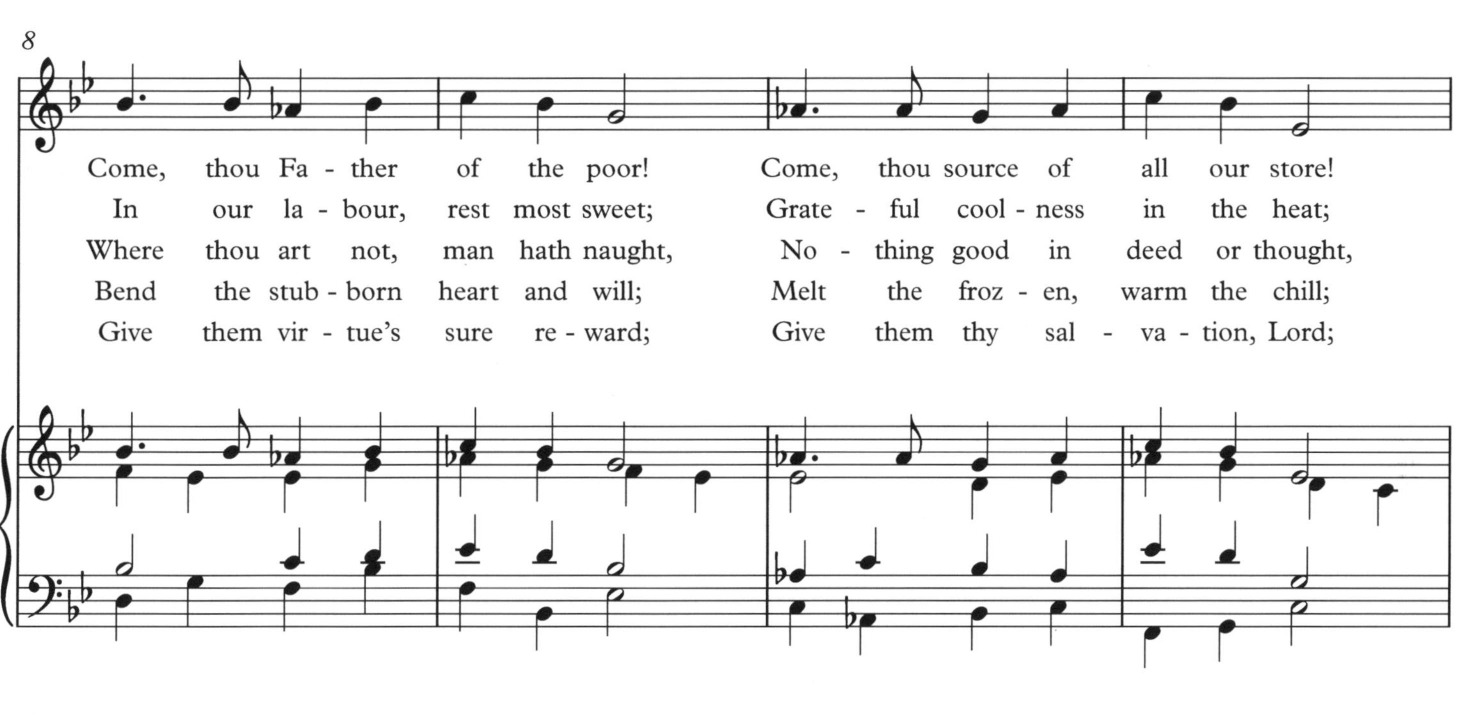
8
Come, thou Fa - ther of the poor! Come, thou source of all our store!
In our la - bour, rest most sweet; Grate - ful cool - ness in the heat;
Where thou art not, man hath naught, No - thing good in deed or thought,
Bend the stub - born heart and will; Melt the froz - en, warm the chill;
Give them vir - tue's sure re - ward; Give them thy sal - va - tion, Lord;

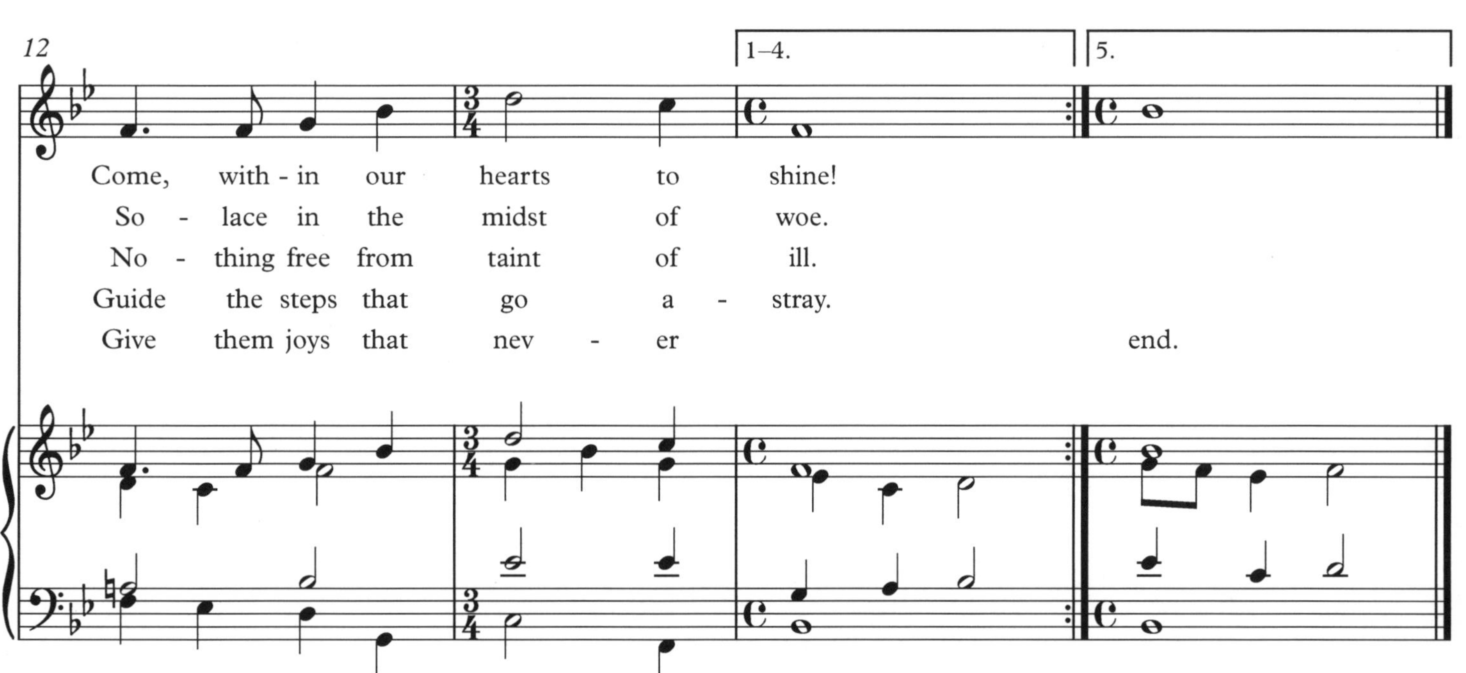
12
1–4.
5.
Come, with - in our hearts to shine!
So - lace in the midst of woe.
No - thing free from taint of ill.
Guide the steps that go a - stray.
Give them joys that nev - er end.

Commissioned by the Association of Anglican Musicians Conference
and dedicated to the AAM 2000 Palm Beach Conference

Variations on 'Palm Beach'

GERRE HANCOCK

I: Foundations 8', 4', III/I, II/I
II: Foundations 8', 4'
III: Foundations 16', 8', 4'
Ped.: Foundations 16', 8', III/Ped., II/Ped.

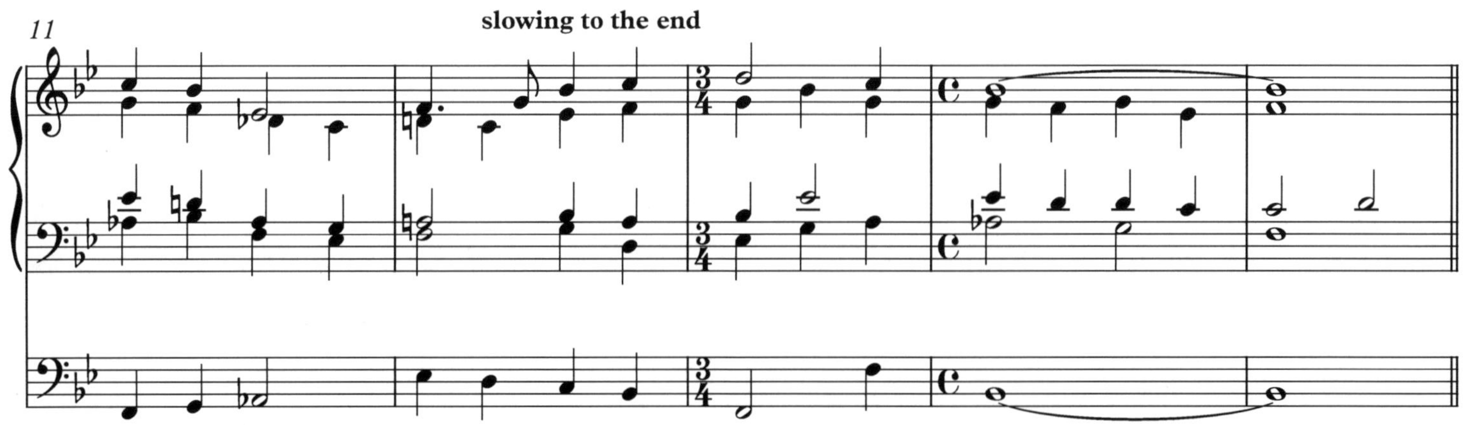

I

II: Solo 8'
III: Foundations 8'
Ped.: Foundations 16', 8'

II

I: Flutes 8', III/I, II/I
II: Flutes 8'
III: Flutes 8'
Ped.: Flutes 16', 8', III/Ped., II/Ped.

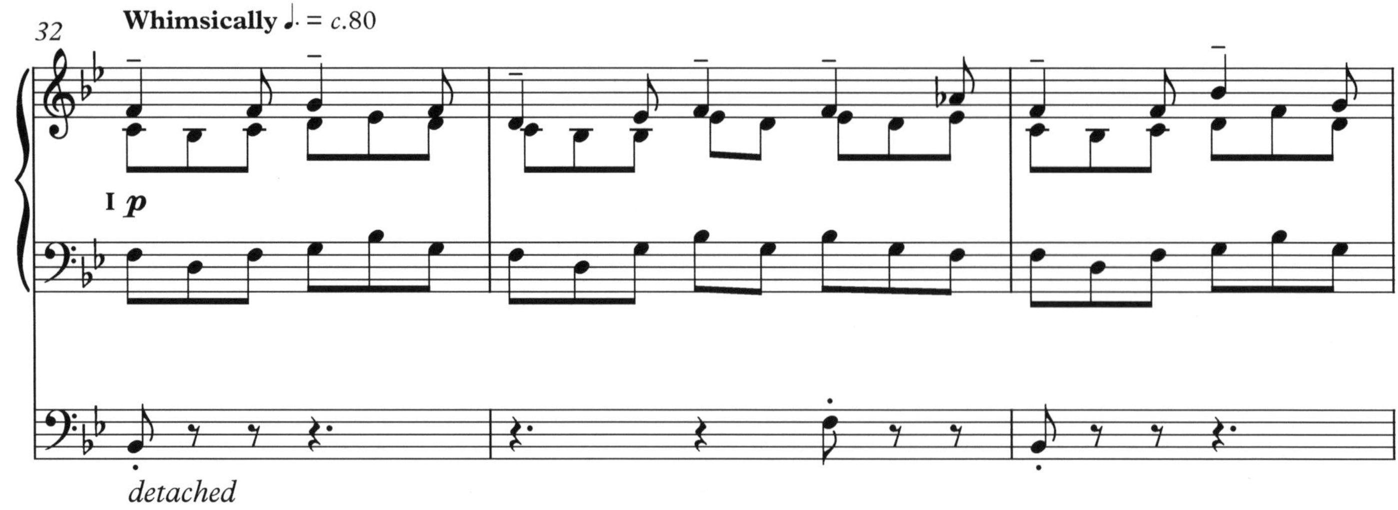

41

44

47
no rit.

III

II: Strings & Celeste 8', III/II
III: Flute 16', Strings & Celeste 8'
Ped.: Solo 4'

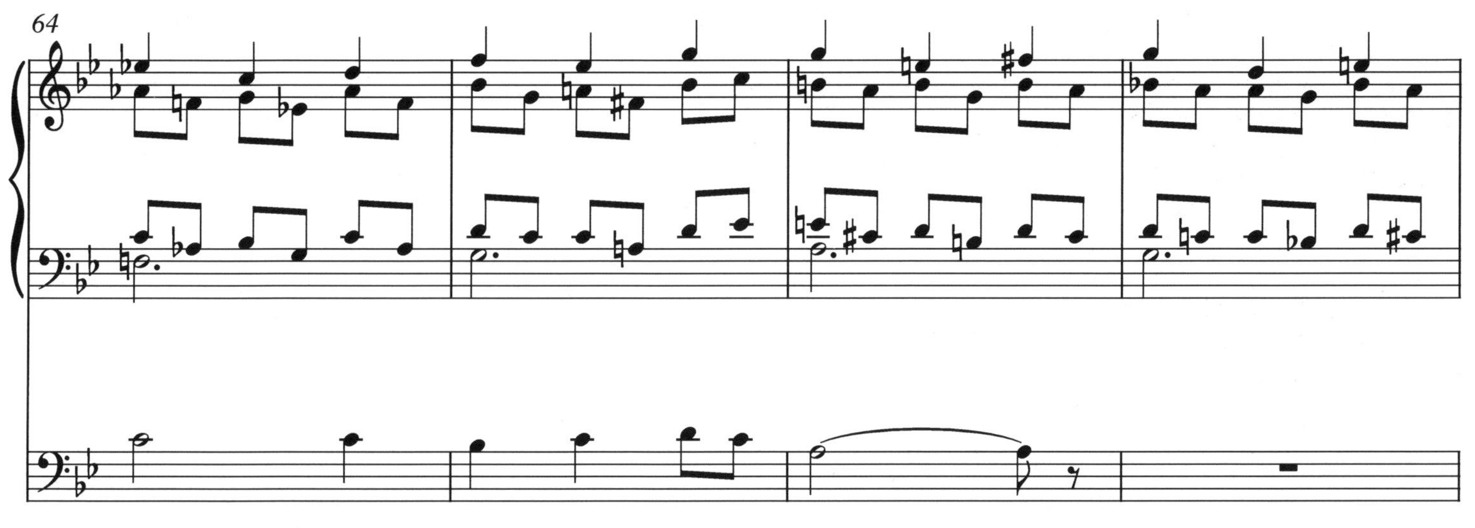
64

68

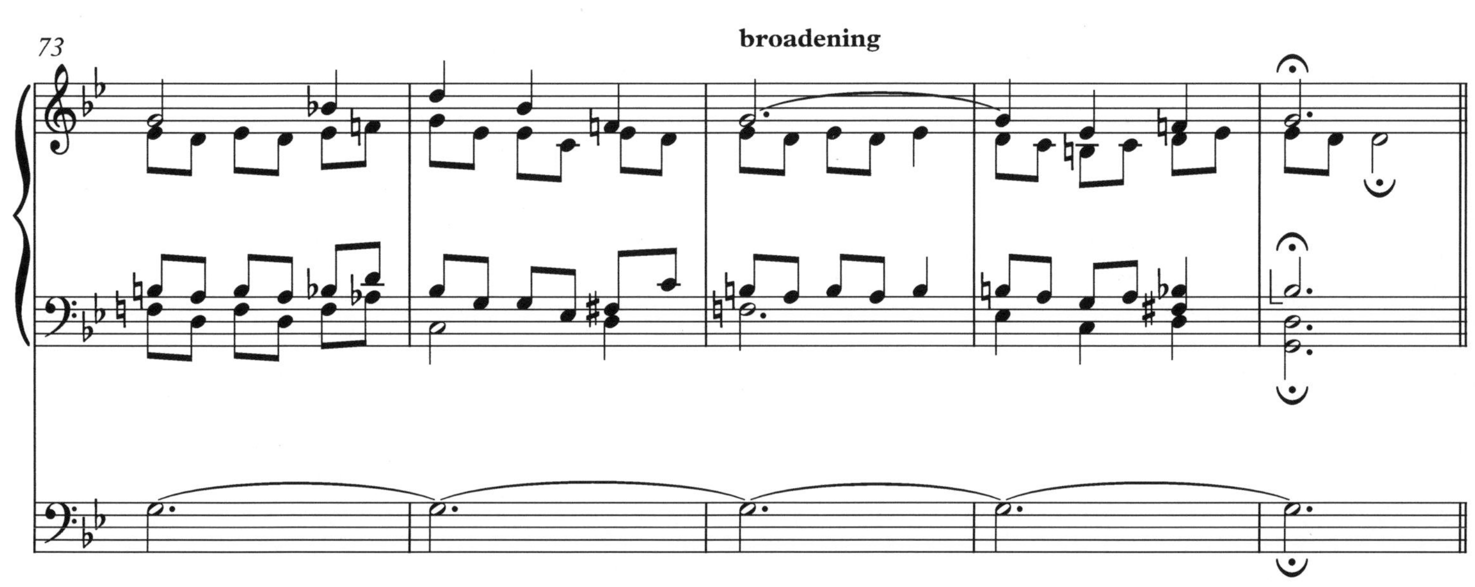
73
broadening

IV

I: Foundations 16', 8', 4', Mixture, Reeds 16', 8', III/I, II/I
II: Foundations 16', 8', 4', Mixture, Reeds 16', 8'
III: Foundations 16', 8', 4', Mixture, Reeds 16', 8'
Ped.: Foundations 32', 16', 8', 4', Mixture, Reeds 16', 8', III/Ped., II/Ped.

89
92
95
slowing
slower to the end
98

Three Cincinnati Improvisations

GERRE HANCOCK
transcribed by Todd Wilson

I. Improvisation on 'Lobe den Herren'

Sw.: Oboe
Pos.: Flutes 8', 1', or other clear 'gap registration'
Ped.: Clear 16', 8'

10
13
16
19

22
26
29
32
3

35
3
3
3
3
38
3
3
3
3
40
3
3
3
3
3
42
3
3
3
3
3

44
46
49
51
rit.

II. Improvisation on 'Grand Isle'

Sw.: Flutes 8', 4'
Gt.: Trumpet 8'
Pos.: Cornet V
Ped.: Flutes 16', 8'

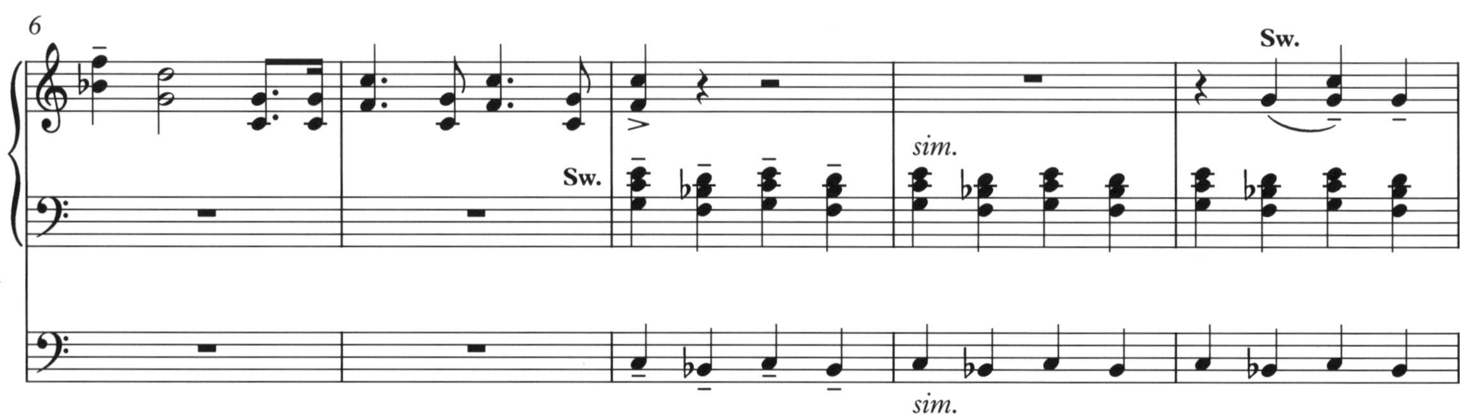

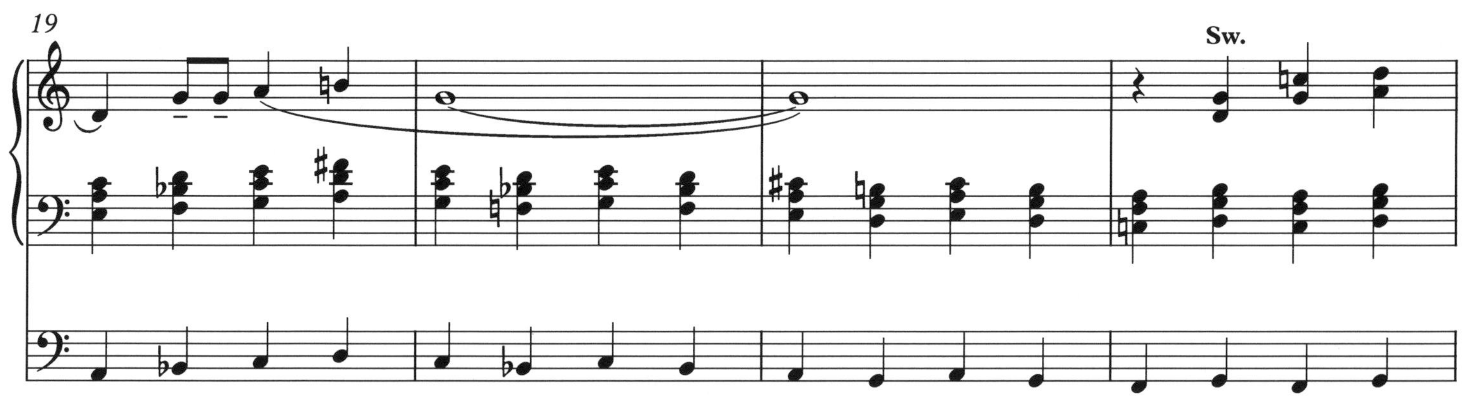
19
Sw.

23
Gt.
3

27
3

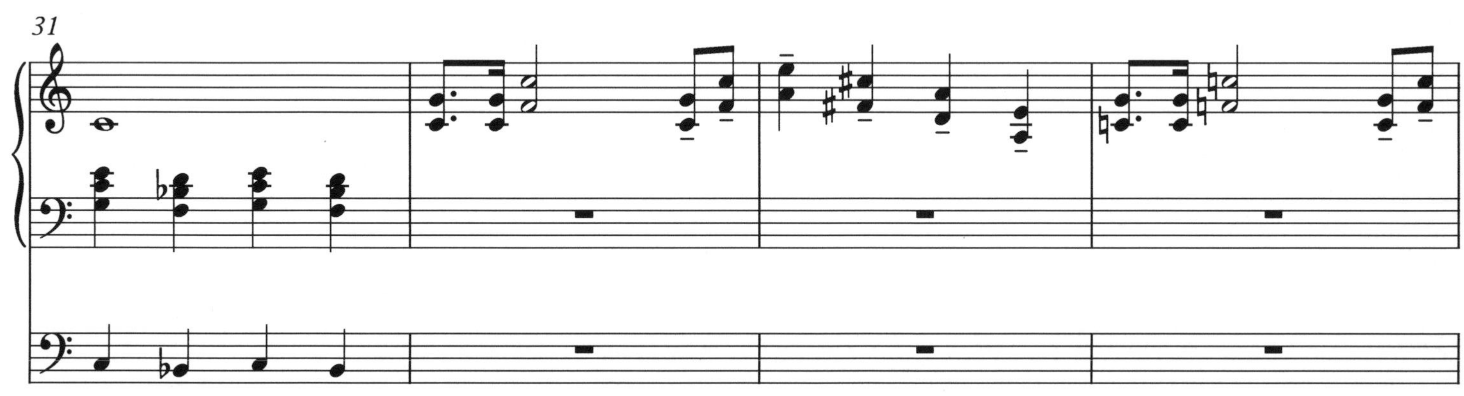
31

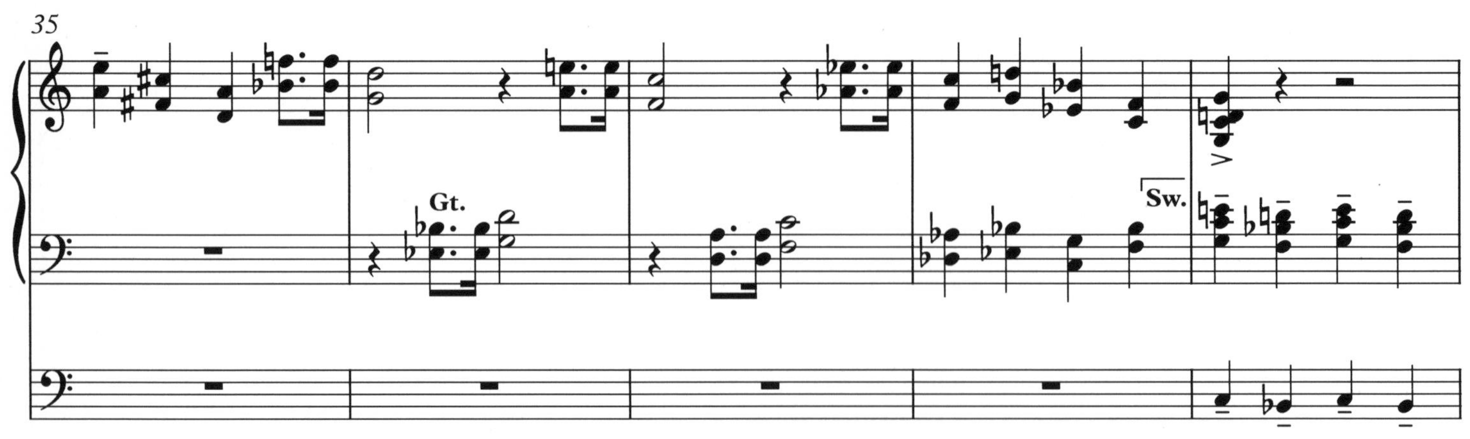
35
Gt.
Sw.

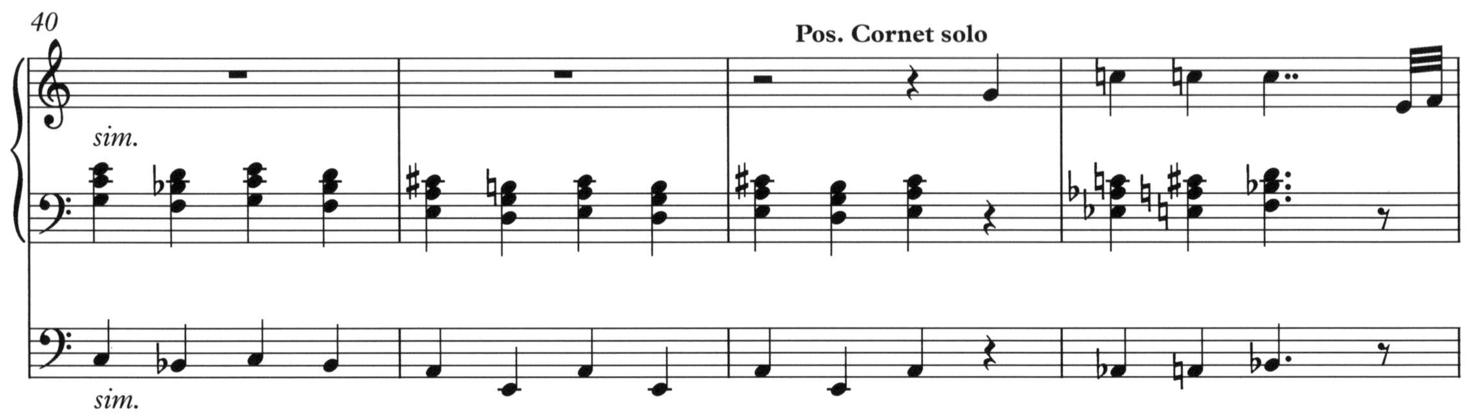
40
Pos. Cornet solo
sim.
sim.

44
3
3

48
3
3
3

52
3
56
Gt. Trumpet
60
Gt.
sim.
64
Sw.
3
Sw.

III. Improvisation on 'Ar hyd y nos'

Sw.: Flute 8', Strings, Celeste
Gt.: Warm Foundations 8', Sw./Gt.
Ped.: 16', 8', Sw./Ped.

a tempo
22
Solo Reed (optional)
Gt.
26
30
Gt.
Gt.
Ch. + Sw.
[add Sw. Reeds, box closed]
Sw. box
smooth dim. over
4 bars
35
[reduce gradually
to Flute Celeste]
Ch.
pppp
[Gt. 8's, Sw. + Ch. 8's with Celeste]
+ 32'